Rick and Morty™

THE OFFICIAL
COLORING BOOK

SOMETIMES SCIENCE IS MORE ART THAN SCIENCE

INSIGHT
EDITIONS
San Rafael • Los Angeles • London

T0052013

SCHWIFTY

WE'RE HERE
WE'RE SHEER
WE WILL NOT BE
IGNORED
LEGAL

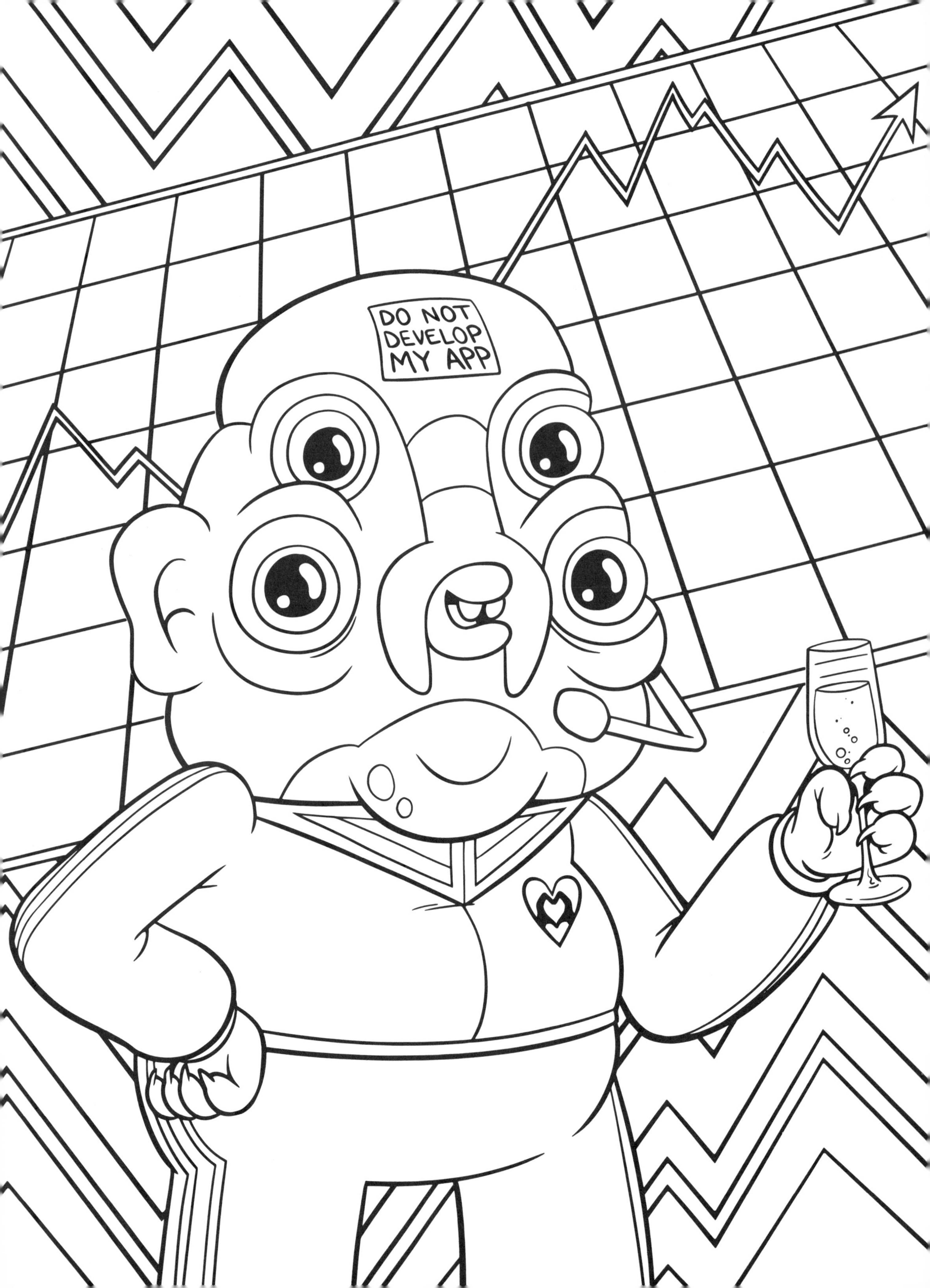
DO NOT DEVELOP MY APP

Professor-
Poopybutthole
Ooowee
π=3.14
(y+A)=2/3A
c=πr2

Merry
Christmasssssss

SSSSS
SSSS!!

CLONE BETH
BETH

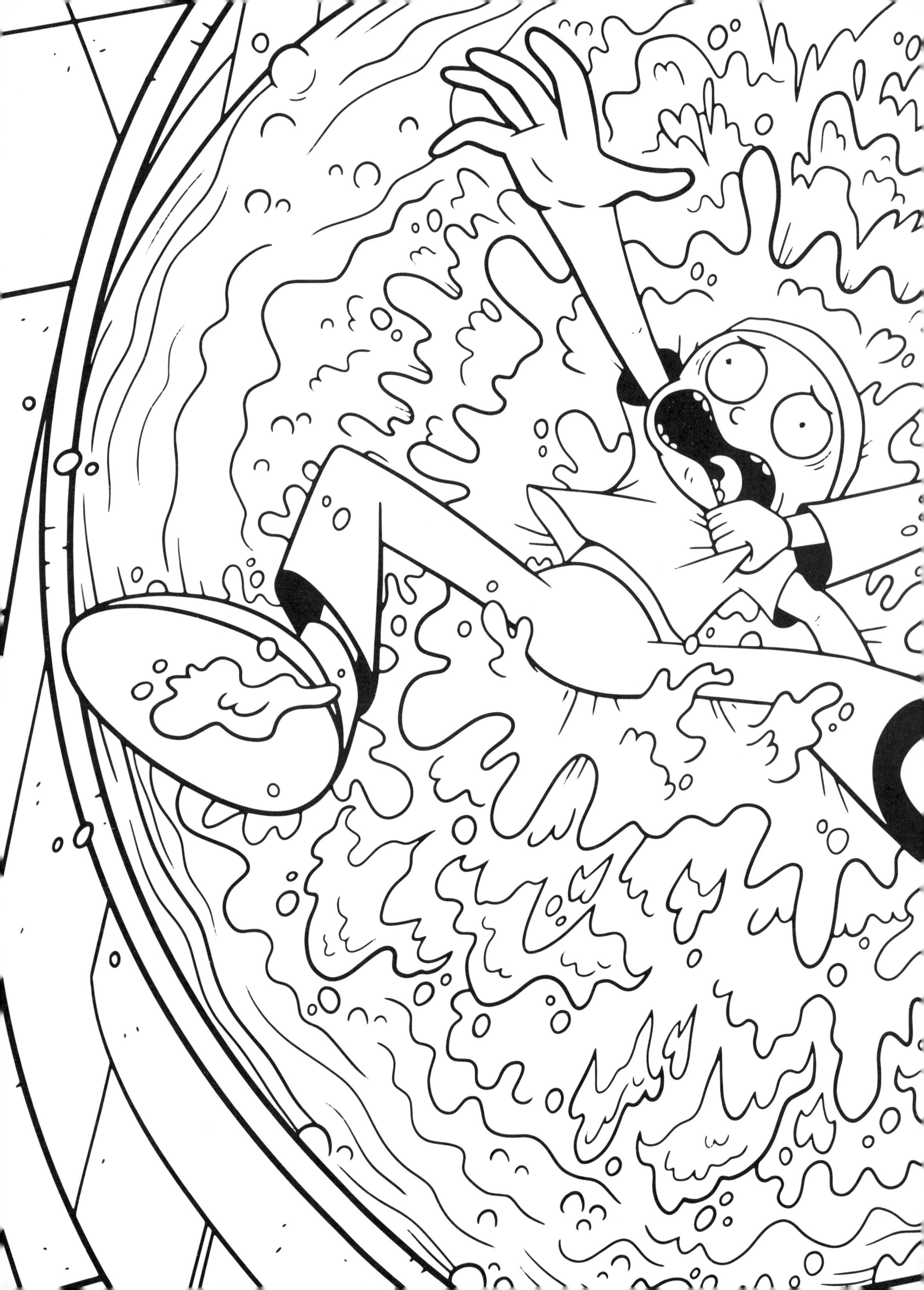

HANDS OFF!

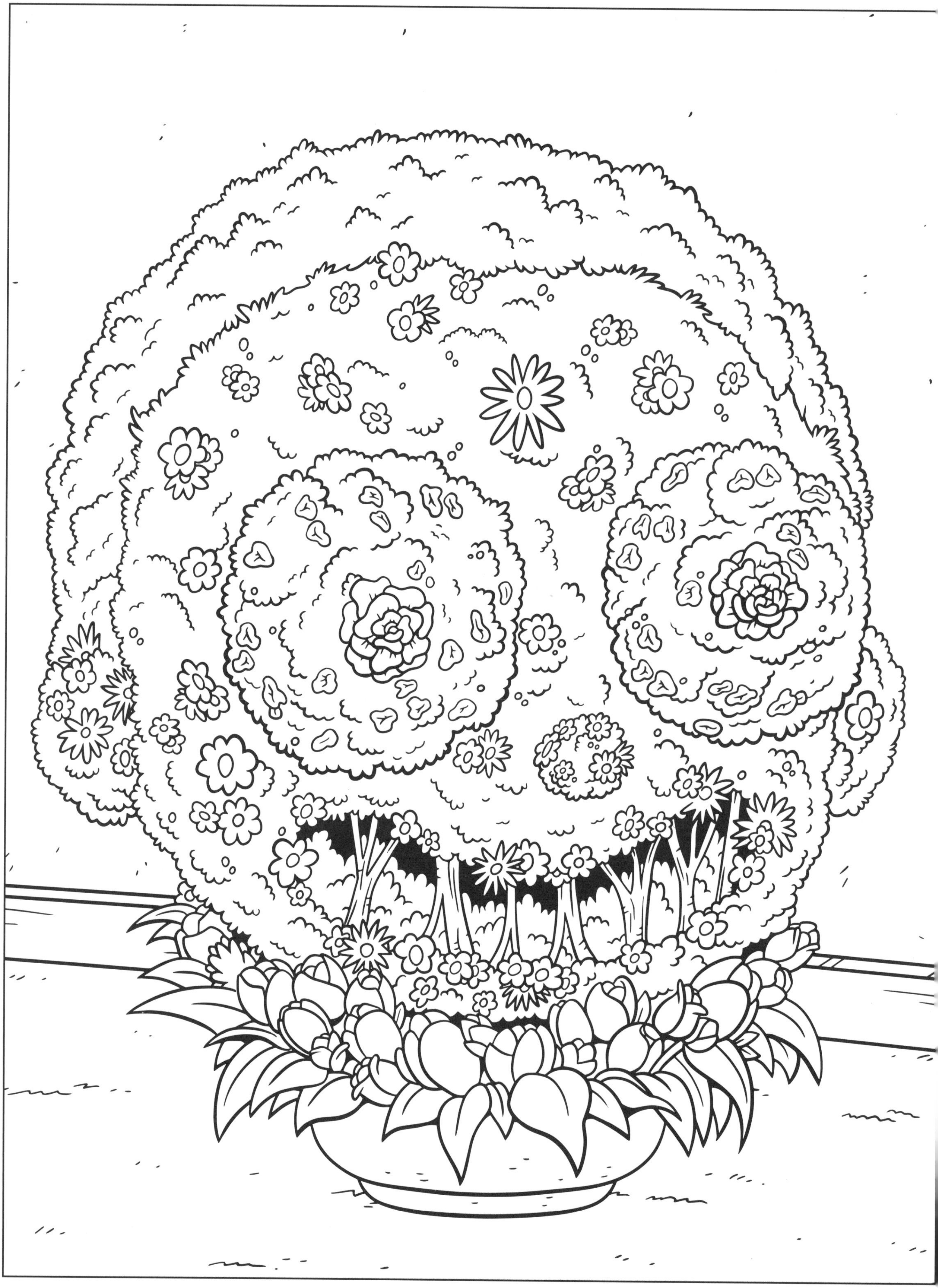

CITADEL
NEWS